More of

THE
REAL
THING

A Skill-Building Book and Video

That Prepares Students

For College Success

Martha E. Kendall

ISBN 0-945783-11-6

cover design by Alice McKown

Highland Publishing
P. O. Box 554
Los Gatos, CA 95031-0554
U.S.A.
phone (408) 353-5756
fax (408) 353-3388
esl@highlandpublishing.com

Preface

More of The Real Thing, like the original video/book program *The Real Thing*, prepares students for the mainstream curriculum at an American college. *More of The Real Thing* contains sixteen authentic college classes, each ten to fifteen minutes long. The skill-building book teaches students how to learn in these classes, which have been selected from a wide range of disciplines beyond those included in the original series.

More of The Real Thing shows conventional lectures as well as classes with student-centered instruction. For example, in the second unit, students sit in a circle and discuss their strategies for preparing for an exam. In another unit, students develop guidelines for working in small groups. In the last unit, a student describes his experience doing a Service Learning project.

Students practicing with *More of The Real Thing* observe spontaneous classroom behavior. Learners participate actively and assert their own opinions, behaviors valued by most professors at American colleges.

Pre-listening activities in the book prepare students for the taped classes. During the first two lectures, students are guided in their listening, focusing on information needed to answer comprehension questions. In the third unit students analyze an example of notes. The fourth unit coaches them in taking their own. In subsequent units, students use their notes to answer questions about each class. Eventually they examine outlines and finally develop their own.

Every unit directs students in responding to the lecture: what to do with the information and how to predict what the professor expects them to know. The book suggests strategies for developing vocabulary, and it helps students become aware of and maximize their preferred learning styles. Every unit concludes with writing topics that relate to the class.

Many oral activities for small groups prompt students to listen attentively to each other, because the individuals and groups are accountable for completing their tasks. In group interaction students develop cooperative social skills needed in many academic and professional settings. In the final unit, students develop evaluation criteria for oral presentations and assess each others' efforts, excellent preparation for doing evaluations in the work world.

Practicing with *More of The Real Thing* builds learners' skills and confidence. It serves as a much-needed bridge for students in advanced courses of English as a Second Language as they prepare to move into the mainstream curriculum. Other learners also benefit from *More of The Real Thing*. Motivated students may perform poorly because of their anxiety about losing face in front of their peers and professors. Instead of suffering from fear of the unknown, learners can practice with these units and gain familiarity with classroom expectations. Some bright students fail because they lack effective study skills. Practicing with *More of The Real Thing* helps them develop their potential. It also encourages students to take full advantage of academic resources designed to help them succeed.

More of The Real Thing can be used anywhere; it does not presuppose residence in the United States. It is appropriate in an advanced course in English as a Second Language, a College Orientation Program, a General Study Skills class or an individualized lab. (Lab users may disregard each unit's section called "Things to Do and Discuss.") Instructional support materials include an Answer Key and Video Transcript.

Depending on students' needs, instructors may choose to show a lecture once for general comprehension, and then replay it, stopping it every few minutes to ask students to summarize what was said, predict what will come next, check their notes for accuracy, respond to questions from the book, or to ask their own questions.

Faculty across the United States and abroad have reported additional uses for *The Real Thing*, all of which apply to *More of the Real Thing* as well. Three of the most frequently described uses include (1) assessment: students' level of comprehension of selected classes serves as a placement tool; (2) faculty development: instructors study and learn from the teaching styles revealed in these varied units; (3) counseling: students interested in particular majors or careers watch appropriate units in order to preview what the courses might be like.

The Real Thing is meeting the needs of thousands of students. I am pleased that *More of The Real Thing* offers them additional opportunities to develop skills essential for success at American colleges and universities.

I thank all the instructors and students who allowed me to tape them in action; in addition, special thanks to the faculty who provided me with copies of their quizzes, handouts, work sheets, and surveys: Madeline Adamczeski, Sharon Antonelli, Allison Connor, Pete D'Eliscu, Kevin Frey, Jimmyle Listenbee, Jim Potterton, Judy Rookstool, and Priscilla Santos. All of you ARE *The Real Thing*.

Martha E. Kendall
San Jose City College

Table of Contents

Your Education Plan
Guidance

Priscilla Santos

I. Before Class

To prepare for a lecture, try to anticipate topics it is likely to cover. Before class, review vocabulary related to the subject.

An "Education Plan" will include a time line or schedule for courses you will take.

To help you understand this lecture, preview this vocabulary relating to college courses and requirements.

General Education: courses required for a college degree regardless of a student's area of specialization; also called "General Ed." or "G.E."

major courses: classes required for an area of specialization

semester or term: a section of an academic year. Most American colleges organize the year into three semesters. The first starts in September and typically lasts about sixteen or seventeen weeks. Spring semester usually begins in late January and ends in late May or early June. The length of the summer semester varies widely, from three or four weeks to ten weeks. Many students do not attend in the summer.

A full-time student in the semester system usually enrolls in four or five courses during the fall and spring semesters. Students generally earn three units for a course that meets about three hours a week.

Some colleges divide the calendar year into four equal terms called "quarters." As with the semester system, many students attend only fall, winter and spring quarters between September and June.

four-year college: a school that offers a Bachelor of Arts (B.A.) or Bachelor of Science (B.S.) degree after a student has completed four years of full-time study. However, it is very common for students to attend part-time, so they take more than four years to complete their degree requirements.

The four years of college study are called freshman, sophomore, junior, and senior. Some students complete requirements for their freshman and sophomore years at a community college where they earn an Associate's degree (A.A.). Then they transfer as a junior to a four-year school.

The sample Ed. Plan that Dr. Santos discusses includes four years of study at a community college in preparation for transfer to a four-year school. The extra time allows students who have not yet achieved college-level competence to take courses that will develop their skills.

assessment: evaluation. Scores on an assessment test show a student's level of achievement. Based on the scores, a counselor advises the student which courses to take. Students with high scores may skip basic courses and complete their college degree requirements more quickly.

open curriculum: a subject without a specified level. For example, a student may plan to take a math course but not yet know which level. The assessment test will indicate the appropriate level.

tutoring: help from someone who is more advanced in the subject. Tutors are often other students.

II. Comprehend the Lecture

As you watch the lecture, answer the following questions. Whenever you need more time, stop the tape. Rewind it if you want to hear a section again. Listen to the lecture as many times as you wish.

1. What did students do in the last class meeting?_____

_____

2. What is the goal for today's class? _____

_____

3. What two kinds of courses go on the planning sheet? _____

_____

4. What three semesters are listed for each year? _____

_____

5. Which two subjects need to be taken in sequence? _____

_____

6. Which class does Dr. Santos advise students not to take during the

summer? _____

7. What determines how many English or math classes students need to

take? _____

8. What is usually students' biggest fear? _____

9. What subject should students begin as soon as possible? _____

10. How do students know what math course to start with? _____

_____

11. Where are students supposed to go before the next class? _____

_____

12. What are they supposed to ask for? _____

_____

III. Summarize

Use each lecture in **More of The Real Thing** as an opportunity to practice summarizing. Identify the main points, put them in your own words, and then write them in about ten to twelve well-connected sentences. Here is a summary of Dr. Santos' lecture. After each of the other lectures, write your own summary.

The planning sheet lists General Education and major courses required for your degree. The Ed. Plan shows the courses you will take each semester.

You must take English and math courses in sequence. Most people should avoid taking math in summer school because you'll want an entire semester to learn the material.

To find out which English and math courses to take first, you need your assessment scores. They will show which level course is right for you.

Get started with your math and English courses so you can finish the sequence by the time you want to get your degree. Some people are afraid of math courses, but you still need to take them. Don't put them off.

Go to the counseling building and get your assessment scores. Based on those scores, you can select the right courses to take.

IV. Develop Your Ed. Plan

A. Set goals

In order to plan your education, you need to set your goals. Respond to the following questions:

1. Ten years from now, what career would you like to have? It's OK to name several possibilities. If you are undecided about your future, simply pick a career that you might be interested in.

2. What major will prepare you for a chosen career, and what degree is necessary for it? You can get that information from any of the following:

- a counselor at your school
- your school's Career Center
- a professional already working in that field
- a newspaper or government employment department advertisement seeking employees in that career

B. Make a planning sheet

On a separate sheet of paper, make two lists: one for the General Education courses and one for the major courses you need to take for your A.A. degree (at a two-year college) or B.A. degree (at a four-year college). You can get that information by meeting with a counselor at your school and referring to your school's catalog. A catalog explains a school's general requirements and courses; the schedule lists details about course offerings each semester.

C. Complete your Ed. Plan

Now that you know what courses you need to take, organize them semester by semester using the time line below for the next five terms.

An "elective" refers to a course that is not required for General Ed. or for your major, but it does count toward the total number of units required for a college degree. Most colleges require about 120 units for a B.A. On your Ed. Plan, include elective courses you would like to take because of a special interest you have, a hobby, or just for fun.

*Semester*_____   *Date* _____

Course & Number   *Units*

_____   _____

_____   _____

_____   _____

_____   _____

_____   _____

                                          Total   _____

*Semester*_____   *Date*_____

Course & Number   *Units*

_____   _____
_____   _____
_____   _____
_____   _____
_____   _____

                                    Total   _____

*Semester*_____   *Date*_____

Course & Number   *Units*

_____   _____
_____   _____
_____   _____
_____   _____
_____   _____

                                    Total   _____

*Semester*_____   *Date*_____

Course & Number   *Units*

_____   _____
_____   _____
_____   _____
_____   _____
_____   _____

                                    Total   _____

*Semester*_____   *Date*_____

Course & Number   *Units*

_____   _____
_____   _____
_____   _____
_____   _____
_____   _____

                                    Total   _____

V. Things to Do and Discuss

1. On a slip of paper, write two definitions: one for what "happiness" means to you, and one for "success." Put the papers in a box and shuffle them. Then, have students draw the papers and read the definitions aloud. Discuss whether education will play a role in attaining either or both. To what extent do you think a person's cultural background affects ideas about success and happiness?

2. Plan an interview with someone who holds a job that interests you. With a partner or in small groups, list questions to ask. Set up an appointment for your interview. Report back to your class how the interview went, and summarize the answers to your questions.

3. If you are not already enrolled at an American college, or are planning to transfer, select several schools to research. Information sources include the internet, college catalogs available at a library, or a guidance counselor. Share your findings with your classmates.
    Consider these factors:
    - admission policies: Is it hard or easy to gain acceptance?
    - tuition: How much does it cost to attend?
    - scholarships: What are the eligibility requirements for these financial gifts?
    - location and housing: Is it easy to get there? Is nearby housing affordable?
    - reputation: Is the college well-known and respected?
    - the size of the college: How many students attend?

4. Imagine that a twenty-one-year-old says, "I have to work to support myself, so I can only attend college part-time. It might take me ten years to earn a college degree! I don't know if it's worth the effort." What are some possible responses? Try role-playing answers given by this person's current employers, parents, siblings, friends, and a sweetheart.

5. Think of something you planned in your life, and explain how the plan did or did not work out as you expected. Your example may be humorous or serious. What did you learn from the experience?

6. Consider these familiar sayings as they apply to your future plans:

*   Look before you leap.

*   Give a man a fish, and he eats for a day. Teach him how to fish, and he eats for the rest of his life.

*   Every journey begins with one step.

*   "The best laid plans of mice and men often go awry."
    (adapted from the poetry of Robert Burns)

VI. Write

1. Many college applications require that students write a two-page personal statement. As practice for your admission into the next higher level of education, compose a two-page paper telling about yourself and your goals .

2. Write a paper comparing your education with that of your parents.

3. Any of the topics in "V. Things to Do and Discuss" can be developed into compositions.

2

How to Learn
Study Skills

Sarita Tamayo

I. Student-Centered Instruction

Instead of giving students information that they are expected to memorize, many professors offer student-centered instruction. In this type of learning environment, the students—not the teacher—provide the focus for the class. Students are expected to be active participants who generate their own ideas.

Dr. Tamayo does not lecture to her students. She asks questions that stimulate their learning. In classes such as this, pay attention not only to what the professor says, but also to students' comments.

Be ready to participate. If the professor asks for your opinion, she is not expecting you to repeat ideas she has already given. Come up with your own.

II. Comprehend the Lecture

As you watch the lecture, answer the following questions. Whenever you need more time, stop the tape. Rewind it if you want to hear a section again. Listen to the lecture as many times as you wish.

1. What two questions does Dr. Tamayo ask students to keep in mind?

_____

_____

2. What is the most important skill you gain in college? _____

_____

3. How does the first student who responds say he studies? _____

_____

4. How does the next student say she studies? _____

_____

5. How does the next student say she studies? _____

_____

6. What parts of a book does Dr. Tamayo recommend reading if you do

not have time to read the whole thing? _____

_____

7. How does the next student say he studies? _____

_____

8. What style of learning relates to his approach? _____

_____

9. How does the next student say she studies? _____

_____

10. What two types of memory does Dr. Tamayo mention? _____

_____

11. What type of learner might benefit from drawing pictures and charts?

_____

12. What factor is a key part of all studying? _____

13. How does the next student say he studies? _____

_____

14. What learning style makes listening to a recording helpful? _____

_____

15. List six resources in the classroom: _____

_____

_____

16. What are at least two advantages of study groups? _____

_____

17. What should study group members exchange so they can communi-

cate? _____

18. What is the first thing the groups are supposed to do? _____

_____

19. What are the groups to give Dr. Tamayo? _____

_____

20. What will Dr. Tamayo give to the groups? _____

_____

III. Summarize

Write a summary that includes the main ideas covered in Dr. Tamayo's class. Identify the key points made, put them in your own words, and then write them in about ten to twelve well-connected sentences.

IV. How Do You Learn?

A. Learning styles

Most people learn in various ways. Because repetition is key in almost all learning, some students purposely study the same material using different methods. Becoming aware of the ways that work best for you can improve your efficiency and satisfaction as a learner.

Visual learners use their eyes. They may read and re-read material in many forms, such as a book, their notes, a web site, or a graph.

Manual learners use their hands. To activate their finger memory, they may make a model, type information on a keyboard, or write and re-write material by hand.

Auditory learners use their ears. They may listen to a recording, speak out loud to themselves or others, or make up sayings that help them remember things.

Which approach to learning is primary in each of these examples? Write *V*, *A*, or *M* on the line provided.

V - Visual   A - Auditory   M - Manual

_____1. "When I learn vocabulary, I recite the word and its definition."

_____ 2. "I read flash cards while I ride on the bus to school."

_____ 3. "I print and study information from the internet that is related to the topic."

_____ 4. "I recopy my class notes."

_____ 5. "I record every lecture and listen to it when I'm commuting."

_____ 6. "When my friends and I have lunch together after class, we talk about what the professor said."

_____ 7. "I copy everything the professor writes on the board."

_____ 8. "I make stacks of note cards that I arrange and re-arrange as I review the material."

_____ 9. "On the phone, my classmates and I quiz each other."

_____ 10. "Using e-mail, my classmates and I ask each other questions."

B. Your preferences

Wanting to learn and being able to learn are two different things. Some students become frustrated if they try again and again to master new material but have little success. Chances are that a different approach to learning could help them. If a method does not work for you, repeating it is not likely to make it work any better.

If you are not satisfied with the speed or extent of your learning, try a new approach. It could be that you are using a strategy recommended by a teacher or a friend, but it might not be best suited for your natural learning style.

Many intelligent people have been identified as having learning disabilities such as dyslexia (a reading disorder) or attention deficit disorders (difficulty concentrating). People with these conditions can learn well, but they learn in uncommon ways. Most colleges have counselors specially trained to help students with learning disabilities.

C. How to talk to your teacher

Dr. Tamayo says it is important to ask questions. To do so, first learn the names of your professors. Most prefer to be addressed by title and last name. "Doctor" is a title for people with a Ph.D., a Doctor of Philosophy degree. If you do not know if your teacher has a Ph.D., you may use general titles such as "Professor," "Ms." or "Mr."

Most instructors welcome questions; in fact, they may think that students who remain silent are not interested in their course.

V. Things to Do and Discuss

1. In groups, have each person explain his/her preferred way of preparing for a test.

2. What factors are important in choosing where to study? In small groups, list criteria. Then ask students to describe their favorite places to study.

3. Many students remember a particularly inspiring teacher who showed personal concern for them, helped them develop enthusiasm for a subject, or gave them new confidence. What teacher made a positive difference in your life? Explain what that teacher did and how you responded.

4. Have each student write on a slip of paper what s/he is going to do in order to be successful in this class. Do not put your names on the papers. Put them in a basket and then distribute them to other students. Have students read the slips aloud and comment on the various strategies.

5. Although education is usually associated with schools and classrooms, most people learn the most important things in life far from an academic environment. Identify something not related to school that you recently learned or discovered. Explain what happened and what you learned.

6. Try this short-term memory game. Let one student assemble about a dozen small objects on a tray. Using a timer, allow the other students to study the objects for thirty seconds. Then, remove the tray and ask students to write down as many of the objects as they can remember. The person who remembers the most wins the game. Ask the winner what strategy s/he used to remember the objects.

7. Plan a three-minute oral presentation. The topic is your advice to a new student. To prepare,

> (1) Narrow your focus to two or three main points.

> (2) Organize your ideas:

>> • Decide on the order in which you'll present them.

>> • Provide at least one example for each idea.

>> • Plan to include visuals, such as writing on the board or showing a picture

> (3) Practice your presentation. Which of the three students below sounds most like you? Which of them uses a way of learning that you would like to try as well?

Student A: "I write the speech down and read it again and again. I read it while I eat breakfast, when I'm on the bus, when I wait for classes to begin, when things are quiet at work, and before I go to bed. Pretty soon I have it memorized."

Student B: "I practice the presentation aloud. When nobody is around, I say my speech. I recite it when I go for a walk, or when I drive my car. Saying it again and again puts it in my memory."

Student C: "I choose things to show during the talk, and I remember what to say depending on the object or chart I will hold up at a particular time. I practice gestures that I'll use to emphasize important points. The props and activities help me remember the topics of my presentation."

> (4) Give your presentation.

> (5) Tell your classmates how you prepared, and comment on which ways worked the best for you.

8. If you are at a college, visit the counseling office and get information about help available for students with learning disabilities. Share the information with your class. If you are not at a college, visit the web site of any American college or university and look for information on programs to help students with learning disabilities.

9. Consider the following as they apply to ways you learn:

- I hear and I forget,
  I see and I remember,
  I do and I understand. (Chinese Proverb)

- "Nothing will work unless you do." (Maya Angelou, American author)

- Practice makes perfect.

- Necessity is the mother of invention.

VI. Write

1. Write a paper describing your most memorable academic success, whether from your childhood or more recently.

2. Write a paper in which you give advice to a new teacher about the best ways to help students learn. Use examples based on your experience as a student.

3. With the exception of number six, the topics in "V. Things to Do and Discuss" can be developed into compositions.

3

Civility in the Classroom
Student Life

Judy Rookstool

I. Strategies for Taking Notes

Bring a pen and notebook with you to every class. At the top of your notes, write the date. If an instructor says, for example, that there will be a quiz on the last two weeks' work, you need to know what was covered during that time.

Skip lines as you take notes. Then, if an example comes up after you first noted an idea, you can insert it. Or, when you're reviewing your notes after class, you will have room to add comments or questions.

Note information if—

- the instructor writes it on the board.
- it is repeated.
- it is discussed at length.
- it is defined.
- the instructor says it is "key," "major," "significant," etc.

Underline or put a star by ideas that seem especially important. Do not try to write whole sentences if a short phrase is clear. Use abbreviations. Many students use symbols such as these to speed their notetaking. Create your own, too.

✱	key idea, main point	↑ (↓)	increases (decreases)
=	equals, is, means	*c/w*	compared with
≈	about equal to	*w/*	with
≠	not equal to	*w/o*	without
<	smaller than	→	causes, leads to
>	greater than	*ex.*	for example
∴	therefore	*etc.*	plus more examples
?	a reminder to find out what a word or idea means		

II. Sample Notes

Dr. Rookstool's lecture generally follows the brief outline she wrote on the board. Here is an example of notes taken during her class. They fill in the outline. Read them as you observe the lecture.

Civility in the Classroom
Monday, October 7

Manners vs. Etiquette vs. Civility

I. Civility — What is it?

   A. Definition

      1. Manners = relating to people daily: "please" + "thank you,"

        going thru doors one at a time

          ex. everyone at table has a place

      2. Etiquette = set of rules for how to act in society

          ex. = correct silverware

      3. Civ. = an underlying principle of respect for others

          ex. = people feel comf. at table

   B. Phil. Theory

      1. Civic virtue

  ?   *a. Aristotle: common values = honesty, loyalty, etc.*

        b. What we owe society

      2. Civil state

        a. c/w civ. virt., on other end of spectrum

        b. Individ. freedoms, rights

II. <u>*Why civility in the classroom?*</u>

    A. Comf. environ't → easier to learn

    B. Model for society

    C. Respect for diversity

    D. Essential on the job

III. *Civ. in the classroom — how would it look?*

    A. No one puts another person's question down

    B. Not talking at same time

    C. Cell phones off

    D. Use English

Answer the following questions about the outlined notes.

1. What does "ex." mean? _____

2. Why was "Philosophical" written only as "Philos."? _____

3. Why do you suppose the student put a question mark by Aristotle?

_____

4. Why did the student underline "Why civility in the classroom?"

_____

5. In a formal outline, all items are grammatically parallel. Why do you

suppose that this outline does not follow that rule? _____

_____

III. Summarize

Write a summary that includes the main ideas covered in Dr. Rookstool's class. Identify the key points made, put them in your own words, and then write them in about ten to twelve well-connected sentences.

IV. Assessing Civility

A. Conversational styles

Behavior that is courteous in one culture may be considered rude in another. For example, speakers of some languages act very assertively during conversations. They may lean forward, speak loudly, interrupt often, and gesture extensively. On the other end of the scale, speakers from other cultures talk softly, carefully take turns, avoid eye contact, and make few gestures.

In your cultural background, what conversational style is usually appropriate? The communication style favored at most American colleges and universities falls in the middle between the extremes of loud, excited participation and quiet, careful turn-taking.

B. A survey of civility

Dr. Rookstool prepared this survey in order to study civility in the classroom. Her research showed that having a different student rate the class's civility each day "brought an awareness of civility in the class." Students who rated their classmates' civility reported more positively about their experience than did students in classes that did not assess civility.

In your class, every day a different student can rate the class's civility, or each student can do so regarding the course in general. If you are not now enrolled in a class, you might fill out the survey based on your memory of a typical class session in a course you have taken in the past.

Directions for the Survey: Observe students in your class and make a general assessment of the civility they exhibit. Write a check by one characteristic for the whole class for each of the ten questions, and make comments when possible.

1. Student listeners face speaker.
    _____ 1. No student exhibits this characteristic.
    _____ 2. Few students exhibit this characteristic.
    _____ 3. Many students exhibit this characteristic.
    _____ 4. Most students exhibit this characteristic.
    _____ 5. All students exhibit this characteristic.

Comments: _____

_____

2. New speaker summarizes ideas of previous speaker.
    _____ 1. No student exhibits this characteristic.
    _____ 2. Few students exhibit this characteristic.
    _____ 3. Many students exhibit this characteristic.
    _____ 4. Most students exhibit this characteristic.
    _____ 5. All students exhibit this characteristic.

Comments: _____

_____

3. Speakers have neutral or positive tone of voice (no sarcasm or "put-downs").
    _____ 1. No student exhibits this characteristic.
    _____ 2. Few students exhibit this characteristic.
    _____ 3. Many students exhibit this characteristic.
    _____ 4. Most students exhibit this characteristic.
    _____ 5. All students exhibit this characteristic.

Comments: _____

_____

4. Listeners and speakers have neutral facial expression (avoiding eye-rolling or smirking).
    _____ 1. No student exhibits this characteristic.
    _____ 2. Few students exhibit this characteristic.
    _____ 3. Many students exhibit this characteristic.
    _____ 4. Most students exhibit this characteristic.
    _____ 5. All students exhibit this characteristic.

Comments: _____

_____

5. Speakers' comments focus on issues, not on a person (no name-calling).
    _____ 1. No student exhibits this characteristic.
    _____ 2. Few students exhibit this characteristic.
    _____ 3. Many students exhibit this characteristic.
    _____ 4. Most students exhibit this characteristic.
    _____ 5. All students exhibit this characteristic.

Comments: _____

_____

6. Speakers' points are supported by reasons ("I agree or disagree because...").
    _____ 1. No student exhibits this characteristic.
    _____ 2. Few students exhibit this characteristic.
    _____ 3. Many students exhibit this characteristic.
    _____ 4. Most students exhibit this characteristic.
    _____ 5. All students exhibit this characteristic.

Comments: _____

_____

7. Speakers take turns (avoiding interruptions).
    _____ 1. No student exhibits this characteristic.
    _____ 2. Few students exhibit this characteristic.
    _____ 3. Many students exhibit this characteristic.
    _____ 4. Most students exhibit this characteristic.
    _____ 5. All students exhibit this characteristic.

Comments: _____

_____

8. Speakers use respectful words or verbal strategies (such as "Please clarify," "I'm unclear about...," "I disagree because..." "In other words, you are saying....").

_____ 1. No student exhibits this characteristic.
_____ 2. Few students exhibit this characteristic.
_____ 3. Many students exhibit this characteristic.
_____ 4. Most students exhibit this characteristic.
_____ 5. All students exhibit this characteristic.

Comments: _____

_____

9. Speakers indicate understanding of another's ideas even if they don't agree ("I appreciate what you say; here's my opinion....").

_____ 1. No student exhibits this characteristic.
_____ 2. Few students exhibit this characteristic.
_____ 3. Many students exhibit this characteristic.
_____ 4. Most students exhibit this characteristic.
_____ 5. All students exhibit this characteristic.

Comments: _____

_____

10. Overall civility rating for this class period.

_____ 1. Not very civil
_____ 2.
_____ 3.
_____ 4.
_____ 5. Very civil

Comments: _____

_____

V. Things to Do and Discuss

1. Working with a partner or in small groups, list at least five ways an instructor can model civil behavior. Compare your list with others.

2. Working with a partner or in small groups, list at least five rules of students' behavior in a civil classroom. Compare your list with others.

3. If you have attended school in another culture, explain some of the contrasts between behavior expected there and in American classrooms. Or, consider different expectations in high school and college classes.

4. One of Dr. Rookstool's students says that people should speak only English in an American classroom. Do you agree?

   To expand the discussion, set up a debate about the use of "English only" in other settings, such as the college campus as a whole, or in government services and operations.

5. Have each person look up a word of his or her choice in the **Oxford English Dictionary** and report the findings to the class.

6. Dr. Rookstool mentions mealtime manners. How do members of your family behave at the dinner table? Have you ever eaten in a different setting and discovered unfamiliar rules of behavior?

7. Discuss the following as they relate to civility:

   - "The right to swing my fist ends where the other man's nose begins." (Oliver Wendell Holmes, Chief Justice of the United States Supreme Court)

   - "Do unto others as you would have others do unto you."(The Bible)

   - Live and let live.

   - Sticks and stones can break my bones, but words can never hurt me.

   - We have two ears and two eyes, but only one mouth. (Vietnamese proverb)

VI. Write

   Any of the topics in "V. Things to Do and Discuss" can be developed into compositions.

4

Teamwork
Project-Based Learning

Judith Bell

I. Use the Board

Try taking your own notes for this class. Skip lines to leave room for corrections or additions you may want to make later.

Remember to —

√ copy every idea the professor puts on the board

√ write main points, not whole sentences

√ use abbreviations, and don't worry about spelling

√ put a ? to remind you to clarify something later

II. Check Your Notes

After you watch and take notes in Professor Bell's class, check whether you have done all of the following:

_____ 1. I wrote the heading "Teamwork."

_____ 2. I wrote the title of the first list, "Good things about teams," or an abbreviated version of it.

_____ 3. I listed four ideas below it.

_____ 4. I wrote "Bad stuff."

_____ 5. I listed five ideas below it.

_____ 6. I put a star or arrow by "Slackers" and "Unfair credit."

_____ 7. I noted that industry expects you to work in teams.

_____ 8. I wrote "Strategies."

_____ 9. I listed six ideas for strategies.

_____ 10. I wrote down the assignment and when it is due.

Now, review your notes. Insert definitions and make corrections.

III. Summarize

Write a summary that includes the main ideas covered in Professor Bell's class. Identify the key points made, put them in your own words, and then write them in about ten to twelve well-connected sentences.

IV. Forming Groups

Judith Bell's students learn many skills as they cooperate to complete a variety of projects ranging from producing a flyer to making a short film. They create products requested by members of the campus community. For example, one group made an informative brochure for the English department about new literature courses. Another group made a video showing how Service Learning benefits students as well as the community.

Similar to the way employees confer with their manager, Professor Bell's students confer with the requestors to make sure their needs are being met.

Group work is an important part of almost all courses. Students may be assigned to work together for one class period, an extended project, or even for the whole semester.

With a partner, list the pro's and con's (advantages and disadvantages) of the following ways of creating groups of three or more:

1. Students choose their own groups.

Pro's   *Con's*

_____   _____

_____   _____

_____   _____

2. Students count off.

Pro's   *Con's*

_____   _____

_____   _____

_____   _____

3. Students with high grades work with students with low grades.

Pro's   *Con's*

_____   _____

_____   _____

_____   _____

4. People who can contribute different skills work together. In industry, teams are usually formed by this method.

Pro's   *Con's*

_____   _____

_____   _____

_____   _____

V. Things to Do and Discuss

1. To practice for a future that is likely to demand professional cooperation, form a team to complete a project.

The team's task is to create a small flyer (one or two pages long) about the class you are taking, or the college you are attending, or a college that you plan to attend. Present your completed flyer to the class and possibly to others as well.

Follow this process in which you (1) determine the skills needed to complete the task, (2) assess individuals' strengths, (3) form teams, (4) make guidelines for your teams, and (5) create the flyer.

1) Determine the necessary skills. Check all that apply, and add any others that you think of:

_____ a) leadership

_____ b) making decisions about content

_____ c) gathering information

_____ d) organizing information

_____ e) writing and editing

_____ f) doing graphics and layout

_____ g) researching printing options

_____ h) working hard

_____ i) being open minded

_____ j) your idea(s):

2) Have each student select three skills that s/he has from the list above. Rank them 1, 2, 3.

3) Form groups consisting of people who have a variety of skills to contribute.

4) With the members of your group, create a set of guidelines about how your group will operate.

5) Make the flyer and show it off to all who are interested.

2. Describe a group project you have done in school or on the job. What worked well, and what needed improvement? Based on your experience, what is your advice to people beginning a group project?

3. Some people say that it is important to get along with co-workers, but it is a bad idea to develop close friendships with people on the job. What are advantages and disadvantages of personal relationships at the workplace?

4. "Synergy" refers to the creative energy generated by people's interaction. For example, a solo musician might play very well, but an ensemble of players is likely to produce a more exciting sound. In other words, the whole is greater than the sum of the parts. List at least five examples of groups that achieve more as a unit than could the individual members working separately.

5. Communication is important in group work in school or on the job; it is also important for friendships, couples, and families. What makes communication effective? In pairs, list at least five elements of effective communication. Exchange and compare lists made by other students.

6. Communication is not always verbal. Hand gestures, facial expressions, and body language can mean different things in different cultural settings. Consider the meanings of gestures and expressions in your native language. If possible, ask people whose native language is different from yours to compare their meanings with yours.

   For fun, you might try a game of charades. Each person takes a turn silently acting out the titles of famous books or movies for your classmates to guess.

7. Do you think there is a connection between a person's playing a team sport well and being able to function effectively in group projects away from the athletic field? List similarities and differences between these group experiences.

8. Consider the following as they relate to groups:
   - Two heads are better than one.
   - Too many cooks spoil the broth.

- Many hands make light work.
- The most efficient committee is a committee of one.
- United we stand.

VI. Write

1. Small groups of friends, sometimes called cliques, play an important role in many teenagers' lives. Describe your experience with such groups.

2. Describe a memorable experience that you had completely by yourself. How would the experience have been different if you had not been alone?

3. Any of the topics in "V. Things to Do and Discuss" can be developed into compositions.

5

Happiness
Psychology

Jim Potterton

I. Take Notes and Use Them

Take notes as you watch the lecture. Be sure to copy whatever Dr. Potterton writes on the board. Also note students' ideas.

Using your notes, answer the following questions. If your notes do not contain all the information you need, watch the lecture again.

1. What area of psychology in terms of research is relatively new? _____

_____

2. What comes to mind when many students hear the word "psychology"? (List half a dozen examples) _____

_____

3. What has psychology traditionally focused on? _____

_____

4. Who is the father of modern psychology? _____

_____

5. In America, it's "life, liberty, and the pursuit of _____

6. In addition to psychology, what is another example of a social science?

_____

7. What book does Dr. Potterton refer to? _____

_____

8. What is the score of the average American who takes the happiness

test? _____

9. What is the equation for happiness? _____

10. What does the S stand for? _____

11. What does C stand for? _____

12. What does V stand for? _____

13. What do babies have at birth? _____

14. What part of the body shows a person's degree of happiness? _____

_____

15. Who studied the natural smile? _____

16. What is the Pan Am smile? _____

17. What is an example of circumstances that can affect happiness?

_____

18. What happens when you put a pen in your mouth sideways?_____

_____

19. What example does Dr. Potterton use to show the effect of "acting as

if"? _____

20. How can anyone increase happiness? _____

_____

II. Summarize

Write a summary that includes the main ideas covered in Dr. Potterton's class. Identify the key points made, put them in your own words, and then write them in about ten to twelve well-connected sentences.

III. Your Happiness

A. Assessing your happiness

Check the number that best describes how you feel on an average day.

_____ 10. Extremely happy (feeling fantastic)

_____   9. Very happy (feeling really good)

_____   8. Pretty happy (feeling good)

_____   7. Mildly happy (feeling fairly good)

_____   6. Slightly happy (a little above normal)

_____   5. Neutral (neither happy or unhappy)

_____   4. Slightly unhappy (a little below neutral)

_____   3. Mildly unhappy (a bit low)

_____   2. Pretty unhappy (somewhat "blue")

_____   1. Very unhappy (depressed)

_____   0. Extremely unhappy (very depressed)

B. Showing your happiness

Selecting from the range of choices below, write the number that comes the closest to the way you would be likely to respond. Compare your answers with other people's. Do you see any differences that may be based on culture, age, or gender?

10. jumping up and down, yelling, crying tears of joy
9. acting really excited, talking fast and loudly
8. exclaiming happily, smiling widely
7. making a few comments, smiling
6. grinning but saying just a little
5. giving a shy grin that lasts a while
4. giving a quick little grin, but looking down
3. showing an expression of interest
2. showing a neutral expression
1. not responding

_____1. You have been accepted at the college you have always dreamed of attending, and you've won a full scholarship.

_____ 2. You have just won ten million dollars in the lottery.

_____ 3. Your brother has returned safely from the war. He is healthy and happy.

_____ 4. You have been given a pair of airline passes that can be used to travel anywhere in the world throughout one full year.

_____ 5. You won a $25,000 gift certificate at the store of your choice.

_____ 6. Your best friend has finished treatment to fight cancer, and tests confirm that s/he is now completely cancer-free.

_____ 7. A major Hollywood producer has offered you a huge contract to make a film on the story of your life.

_____ 8. Without surgery, thanks to modern medicine, you can change your face or body however you might want to.

_____ 9. Your true love loves you back.

_____ 10. Your own idea: _____

IV. Things to Do and Discuss

1. What so far has been the happiest moment of your life? What do you predict will be the happiest day in your future?

2. What kinds of jobs are available for people who major in Psychology? To find out, you can contact a —

- Career Center at your school
- guidance counselor
- Professor of Psychology
- psychologist in private practice
- librarian
- search engine on the internet

3. Imagine that a friend has complained to you about not feeling very happy. Working with a partner, come up with advice about specific things your friend can do to feel better or to get help. Base your ideas on the information in Dr. Potterton's lecture and on your own experiences.

4. Extroverts tend to be outgoing, talkative, and quite willing to share information about themselves. In contrast, introverts are generally quiet and reluctant to talk much about personal matters. Which type of personality do you have? Do you think students with a particular type of personality find it easier to succeed? Why or why not?

5. Consider these sayings:

- Smile and the whole world smiles with you.

- Money can't buy happiness.

- Laughter is the best medicine.

- An optimist believes this is the best of all possible worlds; a pessimist fears this is so.

V. Write

1. The American Declaration of Independence says that everyone has the right to "life, liberty, and the pursuit of happiness." In a paper, explain what you are doing to pursue happiness.

2. Any of the topics in "V. Things to Do and Discuss" can be developed into compositions.

6

Color
Art Appreciation

Allison Connor

I. Take Notes and Use Them

Take notes as you watch the lecture. Then, using your notes, answer the following questions.

1. What does "subjective" mean? _____

_____

2. What does "objective" mean? _____

_____

3. What are some subjective meanings associated with the color red?

_____

4. What are some subjective meanings associated with the color blue?

_____

5. What are some subjective meanings associated with black?

_____

6. What are some subjective meanings associated with white? _____

_____

7. What two different colors do brides wear in Asia and in America?

_____

8. What is a basic color wheel made of?_____

9. What is a rainbow? _____

_____

10. What are the three basic primary colors? _____

_____

11. What are the three basic secondary colors? _____

_____

12. Which media uses a different color system? _____

13. What are its three primary colors? _____

_____

14. Why was the new system developed? _____

_____

15. What are complementary colors? _____

_____

16. What are analogous colors? _____

_____

17. What does "hue" or "chroma" mean? _____

18. How can a color be muted? _____

19. What is a tone? _____

20. What is a shade? _____

21. What does "value" mean? _____

_____

22. Which color is warm, and which is cool? _____

_____

23. What does "achromatic" mean? _____

24. What are some examples of achromatic colors? _____

_____

25. What is the difference between "monochromatic" and "poly-

chromatic"? _____

_____

26. What is the difference between "arbitrary color" and "local color"?

_____

II. Summarize

Write a summary that includes the main ideas covered in Ms. Connor's class. Identify the key points made, put them in your own words, and then write them in about ten to twelve well-connected sentences.

III. Develop Your Vocabulary

A. Get your crayons ready

Doing this exercise may make you feel like a child again, but it serves a serious purpose in addition to being fun. Hands-on learners will find the colors and terms easier to learn after drawing them. Visual learners can study the colors as they draw. Auditory learners should describe aloud what they're doing as they work.

Compare your work with that of your classmates.

1. Draw a color wheel consisting of the three primary colors in pigment, alternating with the secondary colors.

2. Draw two triangles in complementary colors.

3. Draw two squares in analogous colors.

4. Draw two rectangles in monochromatic colors.

5. Draw two ovals in achromatic colors.

6. Draw five different shapes in polychromatic colors.

7. Draw two apples. Color one with local color and the other with arbitrary color.

 apple in local color   *apple in arbitrary color*

B. Prefixes can save you time

Prefixes occur in many words, so memorizing common ones can help you understand new vocabulary more quickly and easily.

Professor Connor refers to the prefix "a", which means "without"; "mono" which means "one," and "poly" which means "many."

Additional common prefixes include:

bi *or* di	two
tri	three
quar *or* quad	four
penta	five
hex	six
oct	eight
deca	ten
sub	below, less than
super	above, more than
equi	equal

Selecting from the list, add the appropriate prefixes:

1. A _____ cycle has two wheels.

2. Two violins, a viola and cello make up a _____tet.

3. The _____agon in Washington D.C. has five sides.

4. Products of top quality are considered _____lative.

5. There are eight notes in an _____ave.

6. An athletic competition with ten events is called a _____thlon.

7. Three rulers make up a _____umvirate of power.

8. A _____liminal message is received below our conscious awareness.

9. When all workers do their share, the job is done _____ tably.

10. A six-sided figure is called a _____ agon.

IV. Things to Do and Discuss

1. With a partner, create three lists, each one containing at least five associations that you have with red, black, and white. Compare your lists with those of your classmates. Which words have the strongest cultural meanings and differences?

2. To explore the meanings of "objective" and "subjective," work with a partner to create two statements—one objective and one subjective—about each of the following topics. Remember that an objective statement is factual; a subjective one asserts an opinion. Compare your statements with those of your classmates. The first one serves as an example.

   (1) time
objective: *This class lasts forty-five minutes.*
subjective: *Time passes quickly when I'm in this class.*

   (2) temperature

objective: _____

subjective: _____

   (3) football game

objective: _____

subjective: _____

   (4) hamburger

objective: _____

subjective: _____

(5) college

objective: _____

subjective: _____

(6) car

objective: _____

subjective: _____

(7) _____ *(a word of your choice)*

objective: _____

subjective: _____

3. Attend a play or movie and assess the characters' costumes. Explain to your classmates how colors were used to enhance the production.

4. Consider the following sayings.

- An apple a day keeps the doctor away.

- There's a pot of gold at the end of the rainbow.

- Beauty is in the eye of the beholder.

V. Write

1. Describe the most beautiful natural scene you've ever observed. Include not only the colors you saw, but also the sounds, smells, and feelings you experienced.

2. Topics three and four in "IV. Things to Do and Discuss" can be developed into compositions.

7

Save a Life
Pre-Hospital Emergency Care

Jennifer Witte

I. Take Notes and Use Them

Take notes as you watch the lecture. Then, use them to answer the following questions.

1. What is the first question the class will deal with? _____

_____

2. What does a baby do if it doesn't want to eat solid food? _____

_____

3. How big is a baby's airway? _____

4. What flipper device protects the airway? _____

5. Where should babies be when they eat? _____

6. What should a woman not do during pregnancy? _____

7. What are some health problems that often occur in babies whose

mothers smoked? _____

_____

8. What kinds of homes hurt babies' health? _____

9. What class can help caregivers learn how to protect babies?

_____

10. What does "back to bed" mean? _____

_____

11. How do you know if a baby's airway is blocked? _____

_____

12. What is one thing not to do if a baby chokes? _____

_____

13. If a baby chokes, what is the number to call? _____

14. What should you tell the person who calls? _____

_____

15. What part of the baby must be supported? _____

16. What should you do first to help a choking baby? _____

_____

17. If that doesn't work, what should you try next? _____

_____

18. If you succeed in getting the baby breathing again, why should you

still let the emergency help come? _____

_____

II. Summarize

Write a summary that includes the main ideas covered in Jennifer Witte's class. Identify the key points made, put them in your own words, and then write them in about ten to twelve well-connected sentences.

III. C.P.R. and Other Shortcuts

C.P.R. stands for Cardio-Pulmonary Resuscitation, which means reviving someone's heart and breathing. The term is often used in reference to helping drowning victims by giving them mouth-to-mouth breathing.

Jennifer Witte encourages everyone to study C.P.R. to learn basic life-saving skills. If you are in an American city, have students contact any of the following service providers which are likely to have information about the availability and cost of C.P.R. training. Report your findings to the class.

- YWCA
- YMCA
- Community Education and Recreation Program
- The Red Cross
- a hospital
- a community college
- life guards at public pools and beaches
- an athletic club

The abbreviation C.P.R. is so commonly used that Ms. Witte does not even explain it. She expects her students to know what she means. Below are other common abbreviations in the academic world.

- **A.S.L.** American Sign Language, used by the hearing impaired

- **B.A.** Bachelor of Arts, or "Bachelor's degree." This degree can be earned after four years of full-time college level study. A person holding this degree is considered a college graduate.

- **C.A.D.D.** Computer-Aided Design and Drafting

- **C.I.S.** Computer Information Systems

- **E.M.T.** Emergency Medical Technician, a trained person who may work in an ambulance or be ready to provide on-site care at athletic events and large public gatherings.

- **E.S.L.** English as a Second Language

- **G.P.A.** Grade Point Average for courses taken.

    Although colleges vary, usually the top grade, A, earns four points; B earns 3; C earns 2, and D earns one. A plus or a minus is worth .3 points. For example, Mary took five three-unit courses and earned these grades:

EMT	A	(4.0)
Math	C	(2.0)
Art	C+	(2.3)
Psychology	A-	(3.7)
English	B	(3.0)

    To calculate the average, add the numbers and divide by five. She has a 3.0 G.P.A.

- **I.D.** Identification, often a card or number showing who you are

- **M.A.** Master of Arts. A college graduate can earn this degree after completing one or two additional years of full-time study.

- **M.L.A.** The Modern Language Association, which issues guidelines for research paper standards and formats

- **P.E.** Physical Education such as athletic conditioning or playing sports

- **Ph.D.** Doctor of Philosophy. A college graduate can earn this degree after completing about three or four additional years of full-time study.

- **S.A.T.** Scholastic Aptitude Test, a standardized test that many colleges and universities require of applicants

- **T.A.** Teaching Assistant, usually a student who has a Bachelor's degree and is working toward a Master's or Ph.D., and who helps to teach an introductory level course

IV. A Sample Quiz

A quiz is likely to cover the information the instructor considers most important. If ideas are written on the board, then you know you may be tested on them.

To prepare for a quiz or test after this lecture, focus on the questions Professor Witte wrote on the board. First, use your notes to answer the questions; then try to answer them without looking at your notes. You might write the answers, say them aloud, or practice doing the life-saving techniques themselves.

In a skills class like E.M.T., some quizzes require each student to demonstrate mastery of the techniques presented. However, because that process is so time-consuming, many quizzes are written.

Here is a quiz based on the lecture:

Directions: On a separate sheet of paper, write a clear, thorough paragraph in response to each of these questions:

1. How does a baby protect its own airway?

2. How can you protect a baby's airway?

3. What should you do if a baby's airway is blocked?

V. Things to Do and Discuss

1. Using a doll, practice helping a baby clear its airway just as Jennifer Witte demonstrates in her class. Then, show the technique to someone who cares for a baby or toddler. Notice the questions asked, and report back to the class.

2. In the United States, anti-smoking education has resulted in decreasing numbers of people becoming addicted to nicotine. In many other countries, smoking continues to be common. Do you or people you care about smoke? Do you believe that it is a good idea to prohibit smoking in public places? Will you allow your children to smoke?

3. Jennifer Witte wears clothing typical for an E.M.T. Other types of clothing are associated with other professions. For example, a surgeon often wears a green top and pants, nicknamed "scrubs." With a partner, list at least five examples of clothing that identifies people in various jobs.

4. Research the career of E.M.T. What are the educational requirements, working conditions, salary, availability of positions, and the chances for promotion?

5. Working with a partner, list at least five criteria for choosing a caregiver for an infant. Compare your list with those created by your classmates. Organize them into one that includes about ten of the most important ideas. Show the list to anyone you know who has an infant or might be caring for one.

6. Ideas about good child-rearing practices often change, especially regarding foods and diet. In small groups, have each student describe something that his/her family used to eat until they learned that it wasn't healthy, as well as something new that they have added to their diet.

7. Consider the following sayings:

- An ounce of prevention is worth a pound of cure.
- You are what you eat.
- It's as easy as taking candy from a baby.
- One man's meat is another man's poison.

VI. Write

Except for number one, any of the topics in "V. Things to Do and Discuss" can be developed into compositions.

8

The Globe
Geography

Ken Baurmeister

I. Be Prepared

In this college-level class, Professor Baurmeister assumes his students know basic geometry.

To increase your chance for academic success, if your assessment scores place you in developmental, pre-college math and/or English, avoid enrolling in courses that require college-level skills.

A counselor can advise you about appropriate courses to take while you work on your math and/or English.

II. Take Notes and Use Them

Take notes as you watch the lecture. Then, use them to answer the following questions.

1. What information would have made Columbus decide not to sail?

_____

2. What does the prefix "geo" mean? _____

3. What does the suffix "ography" mean? _____

4. In what country did the first geographer live? _____

5. On what day did he notice the sun was directly above him? _____

_____

6. What was his name? _____

7. On what day were the shadows longest? _____

8. How did he travel to do his research? _____

9. What city did he go to? _____

10. What unit measured the distance he traveled? _____

11. What geometric shape did he use? _____

12. Using a simple formula, what was he able to figure out? _____

_____

13. Where was this information stored? _____

_____

14. What happened to the information? _____

15. How many degrees are in a circle? _____

16. What is the circumference of the moon? _____

17. Why was Martin Luther persecuted? _____

_____

18. Why was Galileo persecuted? _____

_____

III. Summarize

Write a summary that includes the main ideas covered in Ken Baurmeister's class. Identify the key points made, put them in your own words, and then write them in about ten to twelve well-connected sentences.

IV. Apply the Material

A. Take a quiz

Some quizzes ask you to summarize what the instructor said in class. Many ask you to do more than that: you must apply the information to something new.

Because Mr. Baurmeister spends so much time explaining what Eratosthenes did, it is not surprising that this quiz asks you to use Eratosthenes' method in solving a new problem: calculating the circumference of another planet.

Quiz

Eratosthenes knew the length of both his pole (A) and its shadow (B). He determined C using the formula $A^2 + B^2 = C^2$. He drew the triangle and measured the angle between the pole and its shadow, which was the triangle's hypotenuse (C). It was 7.2 degrees.

Part One (four points)

Draw the triangle in the space below. Label the sides A, B, and C, and identify the 7.2 degree angle.

Part Two (six points)

Eratosthenes knew a circle has 360 degrees. He wanted to find out the circumference (X) of the 360 degree globe. His measuring point was 5,000 Stadia (his unit for measuring distance) away from the pole that cast no shadow. He created this equation with degrees on one side, and Stadia on the other:

$$\frac{360}{7.2} = \frac{X}{5,000}$$

$$7.2\,X = 5{,}000 \times 360$$

$$7.2X = 1{,}800{,}000$$

$$X = \frac{1{,}800{,}000}{7.2}$$

$$X = 250{,}000 \text{ Stadia}$$

Based on this example, calculate a planet's circumference if the angle is 6 degrees, and the distance is 50 miles. Do your work in the space below.

B. Draw analogies

Eratosthenes' formula could be written like this: $\dfrac{A}{B} = \dfrac{X}{Y}$

It could also be written as this relationship:

A : B = X : Y   This is read "A is to B as X is to Y."

Word analogies describe relationships in everything from poetry to intelligence tests. Try completing these analogies.

1. mother : daughter = father : _____

2. tall : _____ = fat : thin

3. London : England = Washington, D.C. : _____

4. gallon : quart = _____ : 25 years

5. pyramid : _____ = ball : circle

6. _____: typewriter = automobile : carriage

7. hammer : _____ = screwdriver : screw

8. carpet : floor = curtain : _____

9. viewer : television = reader : _____

10. _____: students = coach: athletes

Now, create an analogy of your own. Then, remove one item, and test whether someone else can determine the missing word.

_____ : _____ = _____ : _____

IV. Things to Do and Discuss

1. Columbus was trying to find a new route to Asia, but he made a discovery that turned out to be even more important: the existence of the New World. Think of examples when you or someone you know about tried to do one thing, but ended up doing something else that had equal or greater significance.

2. Columbus was a risk-taker. With a partner or in small groups, list at least five activities required of students that might cause anxiety. Then, provide suggestions about how each of those activities can be made less stressful. Share your lists with the rest of the class.

3. Mr. Baurmeister gives examples of people and ideas being censored or restricted. Can you provide more examples, either from history or today? When, if ever, is censorship appropriate?

4. Some people say that much of the math they learned in school is of little use to them in their adult lives. On a slip of paper, have each student write down at least three examples of his/her using math in the last twenty-four hours. Put the slips in a box, mix them up, and then read the slips aloud. Do most people use math for similar purposes, or do you see a lot of variety?

Mr. Baurmeister uses geometry in his profession. Explain why you expect that math will or will not be important in your professional and/or personal life after you have completed your formal education.

5. Find your home town on the globe. Prepare a short presentation that includes the following information about it. You might also bring objects and pictures to show or pass around.

- location
- climate
- population
- cost of living

- recreational opportunities
- cultural places of interest
- educational facilities
- pace of life

7. Consider the following familiar sayings:
- Nothing ventured, nothing gained.
- Don't make a mountain out of a mole hill.
- The grass always looks greener on the other side of the fence.
- Some people can't see the forest for the trees.

VI. Write

1. Describe the most unusual natural place that you have ever seen. You might choose to write about it because of its size, strangeness, symbolic significance, or any other reason why you consider it to be extraordinary.

2. Any of the topics in "V. Things to Do and Discuss" can be developed into compositions.

9

The Binary System
Computer Information Systems

Clem Lundie

I. Meet Prerequisites

A prerequisite (requirement) for students' admission to many introductory courses in Computer Information Systems is the completion of introductory algebra. In this lecture, Professor Lundie mentions mathematical terms that he assumes his students know, such as "theorems" (mathematical rules or laws) and "quadratic equations" (equations containing a single variable of degree 2).

If you are not sure whether you have met the prerequisites for a class, check with a counselor before you register for it.

II. Take Notes and Use Them

Take notes as you watch the lecture. Then, use them to answer the following questions.

1. What number system is used in normal interactions throughout the

world? _____

2. If compared to lights, what would represent the binary system?

_____

3. What two numbers are in the binary system? _____

4. At what speed do electrons travel? _____

5. What rules apply to both the decimal and binary systems? _____

_____

6. What is any number to the zero power? _____

7. In the decimal numbering system, what is the highest four-digit

number? _____

8. In the binary system, what is one plus one? _____

_____

9. In the binary system, what is always the first weighted digit? _____

10. In the binary system, what is the second weighted digit? _____

11. Which system—the decimal or binary—uses more digits to represent a

number? _____

12. What is the base indicator for the binary system? _____

13. For what system do you not need to indicate the base? _____

_____

14. In the binary system, when a one is added to a one, what is left in the

current column? _____

III. Summarize

Write a summary that includes the main ideas covered in Clem
Lundie's class. Identify the key points made, put them in your own words,
and then write them in about ten to twelve well-connected sentences.

IV. Need Help? Just ask!

To see if you understand the material, try this short quiz.

1. Write the number 7 as a binary number: _____

2. Write the binary number 10101 as a decimal number: _____

If you are confident that you know the answers, explain to a partner or to the class how you arrived at 111 for the first question and 21 for the second.

For some students, learning the binary system comes easily, but for others, it may be really difficult. What can you do when you have trouble understanding something in any one of your classes?

The first thing to do is to *ask*...

• *Ask* the instructor for help. If a student falls behind in a course, nearly always the instructor wonders, "Why didn't you come see me for help?" The best students show initiative, actively seeking ways to succeed. The instructor is there for you, but it is your responsibility to ask for help.

• *Ask* in the counseling office about getting a tutor. Most colleges provide free or inexpensive tutoring services. They range from a drop-in center where no appointment is needed and you can get help whenever you have a question, to individual tutors you can meet with regularly several times each week.

• *Ask* classmates to form a study group with you. You can work together to learn new material, complete the homework, and study for tests. Collaboration and discussion help most people learn better and faster.

V. Things to Do and Discuss

1. How often do you use a computer every week? Poll the class. Do you think computer use improves or decreases the quality of your lives?

2. Imagine that a new student at a university exclaims, "Why should I learn how to use a computer? I'll never need one." In small groups, list at least five reasons why it is important to know how to use a computer. Compare your lists with others.

Then, list at least three resources, either on campus or in the community, where a person who is not familiar with computers can learn the basics of operating one. Share your lists.

3. Congratulations! You and your classmates have each won a gift certificate for the computers of your choice. Create a list of criteria to help you decide which computers to get. Then, research the market to see what is available. You can visit stores, use the internet, and ask friends and co-workers. Report your findings to the class. All the information should be true and current. The only made-up part is the gift certificate :-)

4. A controversy has arisen about the appropriateness of violent computer games for children. Do you think kids can be influenced by them in a negative way? Should the games be restricted, and if so, by whom?

5. Individually, or in pairs, look up the definitions of these computer-related terms. Add to the list if you wish. Explain to your classmates what the words mean and why they are significant. During your explanation, try to do more than talk about the term. To help people of diverse learning styles, try to include a visual or a hands-on experience.

bit	download	search engine
boot up	hacker	server
browser	RAM	web page
byte	ROM	web site

VI. Write

1. Any of the topics in "V. Things to Do and Discuss" can be developed into compositions..

10

The Heart
Anatomy

Pete D'Eliscu

I. The Language of Anatomy

Every field of study has its own vocabulary. Most science textbooks provide an alphabetical glossary that defines special terms mentioned in the book. This glossary may help you understand Dr. D'Eliscu's lecture.

anatomy: the science dealing with the structure of animals and plants

apex: point

atrium: an upper chamber of the heart

bilateral: two-sided (*bi* = two; *lateral* = sided)

cadaver: dead body

capillary: a tiny blood vessel

cardiac, cardioid: having to do with the heart (*card* = heart)

carotid artery: a blood vessel that conveys blood from the heart to the head

dehydrated: deprived of water (*de*=removal; *hydra* = water)

diabetic: having diabetes, a disease involving the production of insulin

lobe: a projection or section that is fairly round

lunar: having to do with the moon

mitral valve: a membrane that opens and closes, controlling the flow of blood between the left atrium and left ventricle

pulmonary: having to do with the lungs

septum: a divider

trachea: the passage that conveys air to the lungs

(un) oxygenated: (not) containing oxygen gas

ventricle: a lower chamber of the heart

Dr. D'Eliscu speaks in an informal style. You may find it helpful to review this slang he uses before you watch the lecture.

couch potato: a person who sits around and gets little exercise
croak: to die
puppy: a thing
sucker: a thing

II. Take Notes and Use Them

Take notes as you watch the lecture. Refer to them to answer the following questions.

1. Where is your heart located? _____

2. How big is a human heart? _____

_____

3. What was wrong with the cadaver's heart? _____

4. What is the heart made of? _____

5. What are at least four examples of idiomatic phrases about the heart?

_____

_____

6. What are at least five factors affecting heart rate? _____

_____

_____

7. What is the approximate normal range for number of heart beats per

minute? _____

8. How can you slow your heart rate? _____

_____

9. What can make your heart rate speed up? _____

_____

10. How much does a heart pump in a minute? _____

_____

11. What does one side of the heart do? _____

_____

12. What does the other side of the heart do? _____

_____

13. Why does the right ventricle have a thin wall? _____

_____

14. Why does the left ventricle have a thick wall? _____

_____

15. What will Dr. D'Eliscu do with the students on the track? _____

_____

III. Summarize

Write a summary that includes the main ideas covered in Dr. D'Eliscu's class. Identify the key points made, put them in your own words, and then write them in about ten to twelve well-connected sentences.

IV. Develop Your Vocabulary

Many students are surprised to discover the amount of vocabulary they must learn when they take science courses. How can you memorize so many new words?

Depending on your preferred ways of learning, try several of these strategies to commit a new idea to your long-term memory:

• *Make it matter.* People remember best the information that has significance to them. Find ways to tie new ideas to your own life and to things you are already familiar with. For example, "dehydration" means lacking water. To learn that word, you might say something like this to yourself whenever you are thirsty: "I'm dehydrated. I need to hydrate. I won't go to a fire hydrant. I'll get water from the drinking fountain."

• *Create a gimmick.* For example, to remember the word "septum," which means "divider," you might think about how September divides the summer from the school year.

• *Notice prefixes and roots.* "Bilateral" can be remembered if you recall that "bi" means "two," and "lateral" means sides.

• *Make sound associations.* "Cardioid" means having to do with the heart. "Card-" and heart almost rhyme.

• *Maximize flash cards.* Making flash cards gives you a hands-on experience with the words, as does organizing them into related piles. Read the words and their definitions silently and aloud. Draw pictures to illustrate the words, too.

• *Study with your classmates.* Quiz each other on the vocabulary, both orally and in writing. You could also play charades, silently acting out the words until your classmates can guess them.

• *Be a teacher.* Whether your "students" are actual classmates or your furniture at home, try to repeat the lecture, explaining the vocabulary as you do.

• *Practice.* Select any word from the glossary at the beginning of the unit and create a strategy for learning it. Explain to a partner or the class which word you selected, and how you will remember it.

V. Things to Do and Discuss

1. Dr. D'Eliscu mentions idiomatic phrases relating to the heart. Can you provide more examples about the heart, or any other body parts such as the eyes or head? If you speak a language in addition to English, explain one of its idioms that relate to anatomy.

2. Dr. D'Eliscu says that on a quiz some day his students will link anatomy and poetry. Have each student select a short poem that mentions the heart. Read it aloud to the class and explain its meaning. Be prepared to answer your classmates' questions. After your presentation, you deserve a pat on the back and a heartwarming round of applause.

3. Determine the rate your heart beats per minute by taking your pulse for fifteen seconds and multiplying by four.

4. Sigmund Freud, the father of psychoanalysis, once said, "Anatomy is destiny." He meant that women and men act as they do largely because of their physical makeup; their most fundamental behavior is determined by their biology, not by their upbringing or environment. Do you agree?

5. Explain and discuss these familiar expressions that refer to human anatomy:

> • All brawn, no brains.
>
> • Your eyes are bigger than your stomach.
>
> • Put your money where your mouth is.
>
> • Get off my back.
>
> • You've got the world on your shoulders.

VI. Write

1. Write a paper in which you describe a time that you had to choose between what your heart wanted and what your head wanted. What did you do, and how do you feel about the choice now?

2. Obesity has reached epidemic proportions in the United States, and heart disease is the number one cause of death. In a paper, describe your diet and exercise patterns.

3. Topics four and five in "V. Things to Do and Discuss" can be developed into compositions.

11

Self-Esteem
Child Development

Sharon Antonelli

I. Outline the Lecture

As you listen to the lecture, try filling in the missing words and phrases in this outline. In a formal outline, all elements are grammatically parallel. However, when you are taking notes, you probably won't have time to refine your outline that way. Practice with this realistic example of notes taken on-the-spot using abbreviations and short phrases.

Self-Esteem

Tuesday, February 6

I. *What is self-esteem?*

   A. *Positive*

      1. *Confidence*

      2. *Feeling _____ about self*

   B. *Negative*

      1. *Depression*

      2. _____

      3. *Stressed out*

      4. *Paranoia*

II. Why is <u>self-esteem important</u>?

A. Affects how you act: If you don't feel well,

you won't _____

B. Affects other people: They won't want

to _____

C. Affects the choices _____

D. Affects how you look at _____

E. Conditional vs. unconditional

1. Cond. = feel good about _____

only if things are going _____

2. Uncond. = feel good even if you _____

_____

III. How can adults help kids develop pos. self-esteem?

A. _____ reinforcement

B. _____ model

C. Praise them for who they _____

D. Encourage them to take a few _____

E. Doing things on own ➔ confidence +_____

F. During infancy

1. Close _____ contact

2. _____ = Mothereze

G. Let toddlers explore, but be _____

IV. How can adults improve their _____?

II. Summarize

Write a summary that includes the main ideas covered in Sharon Antonelli's class. Identify the key points made, put them in your own words, and then write them in ten to twelve well-connected sentences.

III. Students' Self-Esteem

A. Assess your self-esteem

Having positive self-esteem can help you achieve what you want in many parts of your life. If your self-esteem is not as high as you wish it were, you can take steps to feel better about yourself.

First, assess your self-esteem. Rate each sentence as it applies to you on a scale from 0-5.

    5 = This is true for me all the time.
    4 = This is usually true for me.
    3 = This is true for me about half the time.
    2 = This is true for me fairly often.
    1 = This is seldom true for me.
    0 = This is not true for me.

_____ 1. I feel that the family I grew up in was loving and caring toward me.

_____ 2. I spend little time wondering what other people think of me.

_____ 3. I enjoy challenges that test my limits.

_____ 4. When people make me mad, I tell them so.

_____ 5. I think I am as good as everyone else, even if I might not have some people's high grades, good looks, or social standing.

_____ 6. I spend little time trying to make people like me.

_____ 7. I am in charge of my life; I am not a victim.

_____ 8. I am at ease with strangers and can make friends easily.

_____ 9. I am happy to be me.

_____ 10. I tell the truth about things that I do.

B. Strategies to build self-esteem

If you want to improve your self-esteem, try these strategies:

1. *Do not compare yourself to others.* In our large world, there will always be somebody with more money, more friends, or more fame. Appreciate the unique person you are, not how you stand in relation to others.

2. *Focus on the positive.* Begin by making a list of ten of your best qualities. Don't be modest! Post the list where you can see it every day. You have strengths, and you can build on them.

When you reflect on recent experiences, give yourself the freedom to enjoy thinking about what you did right.

3. *Be your own best friend.* Imagine that a friend is writing a letter of introduction about you. You write the letter, focusing on your strengths.

4. *Take control of your time.* Keep a log of your activities for a week. Are you pleased with the way you are scheduling your time for study, work, friends, family, etc.? If not, identify realistic changes that you can make so that your life becomes more the way you want it to be.

5. *Set your long-term goals.* Make a step-by-step plan for how to achieve them. Instead of focusing on how much needs to be done, congratulate yourself on each step you take in the right direction.

6. *Seek help.* If you feel unhappy with yourself or your life, see a counselor at your school, religious group, or community agency. Self-doubt makes it more difficult for you to suceed. To make your life easier, let a professional help you get on the right track.

C. Student success

Working with a partner or in small groups, consider the role of self-esteem in determining students' success:

1) List behaviors of a student with high self-esteem:

a) _____

b) _____

c) _____

d) _____

e) _____

2) List behaviors of a student with low self-esteem:

a) _____

b) _____

c) _____

d) _____

e) _____

3) Suggest at least five ways students with low self-esteem might be able to improve their learning. For additional ideas, you might review Unit Two, Dr. Tamayo's class on how to learn, and Unit Five, Dr. Potterton's lecture on happiness.

a) _____

b) _____

c) _____

d) _____

e) _____

IV. Things to Do and Discuss

1. With a partner, list at least five ways a teacher can build students' self-esteem. Exchange lists with classmates, and read them aloud.

2. On a slip of paper, write down a strategy you use to help you cope when you are having a bad day or a bad week. Put the slips in a box, and draw each others'. Read the ideas aloud, and discuss.

3. Some people say they feel better about themselves when they think that they look good, perhaps because they have lost extra weight, gotten a haircut or a new outfit. An old expression said, "Clothes make the man." How much does appearance affect a person's self-esteem?

4. Consider the following:

- I'm OK, you're OK.

- You get only one chance to make a first impression.

- You would worry less about what people think of you if you realize how seldom they do.

V. Write

1. Write a paper about a person you especially admire. It can be someone you know on a personal level, or someone who is famous.

2. Being a good winner can be almost as hard as being a good loser. Describe a time when you or someone you know about won something and handled the victory well—or not.

3. Write a paper explaining what makes a good parent. Use specific examples to illustrate your ideas.

4. Any of the topics in "IV. Things to Do and Discuss" can be developed into a composition.

12

Separate Spheres
Gender Studies

Padma Manian

I. Take Notes and Use Them

Take notes as you watch the lecture. Then, use them to answer the following questions.

1. What does "separate spheres" mean? _____

_____

2. When did this idea begin? _____

3. Where did women work? _____

4. What were women responsible for? _____

5. Where did men work? _____

6. What do we call the person who earns the wages? _____

_____

7. What natural quality did women seem to have more than men?

_____

8. What natural quality did men seem to have more than women?

_____

9. What job outside the home seemed like an extension of women's

natural role? _____

10. What are five examples of feminized jobs today? _____

_____

11. Who does the government most often give money to for raising

children? _____

12. Which parent usually gets custody of children after adivorce?

_____

13. What kind of economy did the U.S. have before the industrial

revolution? _____

14. What social class developed with the growth of cities? _____

_____

15. Which social group came closest to living the ideal of separate spheres?

_____

16. What benefit did some women feel as a result of the idea of separate

spheres? _____

17. Who encouraged separate spheres? _____

_____

18. What is the assignment for next time?_____

_____

II. Prepare for an Essay Exam

To earn a high grade, you need to do more than simply know the course material. You also have to write well about it.

Before any exam, try to anticipate what will be asked. Look over your notes and your textbook, and form questions about the key points you starred or underlined. Practice answering your questions using your notes, and then without them.

Here are directions for a test based on Dr. Manian's lecture:

In an essay, explain the notion of "separate spheres," how it began, and its impact today.

To do well, you need to be sure you answer all three parts of the question. It requires that you explain:

        1) what "separate spheres" means

        2) how the idea began

        3) its impact today

The basic essay consists of the following parts:

Title
This should be a brief phrase that clearly indicates the essay's topic.

Paragraph One, the Introduction
    This paragraph leads into the essay and states the essay's thesis, which is the main opinion the essay will defend.

Paragraphs Two through Four, the Body
    Each of these paragraphs usually begins with a topic sentence. It asserts an idea or reason supporting the thesis. Explanation and examples fill out each paragraph.

Paragraph Five, the Conclusion
    This paragraph restates the thesis in different words, briefly summarizing the essay. The last sentence provides a sense of finality.

The following outline serves as an organized list of reminders about what to include in the essay. Notice how each of the three body paragraphs focuses on one of the three parts of the question. Because the exam time is limited, the writer uses abbreviations and shortcuts to speed the planning process.

Separate Spheres

I. Intro
- *A. Lead in: "A woman's place..."*
- *B. Thesis: The notion of separate spheres began in the industrial era and still affects the United States today.*

II. Define "separate spheres"
- *A. Men & women function separately*
- *B. Women = moral, nurturing kids at home*
- *C. Men = compet., breadwinners*

III. How idea began
- *A. In agrar. economy, home = econ. unit of prod.*
- *B. Rise of indust. → cities*
- *C. Women gain power in homes*
- *D. Ideal praised by pol., church leaders*
- *E. Ideal poss. only for middle class women*

IV. Today
- *A. Teaching*
- *B. Other fem. jobs = nurs., child care, admin. assist., flight attend'ts*
- *C. Gov't $ to mothers*
- *D. Custody to mothers*

V. Conclusion
- *A. Spheres less separate today*
- *B. New version: "A woman's place..."*

Have one student read this essay aloud while the rest of the class silently reads the outline on which it is based.

Separate Spheres

The expression "A woman's place is in the home" reflects a notion of distinct gender roles that began almost two hundred years ago. The idea of separate spheres grew popular when the industrial era began, and it is still evident today.

"Separate spheres" meant that men and women should function in their own unique areas. Women were seen as moral and nurturing, so they were naturally suited to running the household and raising the children. In contrast, men left the home to be the breadwinners. They were considered less moral and more competitive, and better able to bring home the wages.

Before the industrial revolution, the United States had an agrarian economy. Both men and women worked in or near the home. However, in the early Nineteenth Century, industrialization began, and cities grew. Men worked in factories to earn money, and women stayed home to raise the children. This division of labor became the social ideal, praised by politicians and church leaders. Women felt a sense of power in their households. Of course, poor women and those on the frontier were not able to attain this ideal.

The notion of separate spheres is evident in the work world today. Teaching, still dominated by women, was the first job outside the home that was considered acceptable for middle class women. It was seen as a caretaking role that simply extended what women naturally did with their children in the home. Other nurturing jobs are still "feminized," such as nursing, doing child care, working as administrative assistants and flight attendants. Government programs help poor women stay home to take care of their children, and after a divorce, custody is usually awarded to mothers.

Although the notion of separate spheres lingers today, many women are entering the work force in nontraditional professions ranging from business to politics. As the bumper sticker says, "A woman's place is in the House...and in the Senate."

III. What to Keep, What to Delete

The essay above summarizes the lecture. On a separate piece of paper, rewrite the essay, reducing its length from 350 words to about 175. Decide which ideas are most important and which can be eliminated. If you write an essay in class, you may have to leave out many things simply because there isn't time to include everything that you know about a topic.

IV. Things to Do and Discuss

1. Dr. Manian does not give her personal opinion about separate spheres. She presents the information objectively. In small groups, try to reach agreement on whether you think professors should give their opinions, mention only the facts, or do some of both. What should students do?

2. What is the impact on a couple's relationship when both the husband and wife earn wages? If you are not yet married, do you expect you and your spouse will both work outside the home?

3. If you are familiar with roles for husbands and wives in more than one culture, compare them with the notion of separate spheres.
    Or, you might consider generational differences. Is your role as a man or woman different from your parent's?

4. Have you observed separate spheres for men and women in education? If so, does the separation seem fair and appropriate? If not, do you think separating the sexes in school might be a good idea?

5. With a partner, list majors for which you think a course in Gender Studies should be recommended or required.

V. Write

1. Any of the topics in "IV. Things to Do and Discuss" can be developed into essays.

13

American Government
Political Science

Martin Morales

I. Level the Playing Field

If a playing field is level, everyone has an equal chance to perform well. But in academics, as in much of life, the field is seldom level. Students from different school systems are likely to have more or less experience with various subjects.

Depending on where you attended high school, you may have been taught a great deal or very little about the American system of government. Most of your college classmates are likely to be quite familiar with the material. What can you do if you are not?

Before the course begins, meet with the instructor and ask for advice about how you can best prepare yourself. For example, perhaps reading a book written for children can give you a quick, simple overview of a topic. Also, you might start reading the course's assigned textbook before the semester begins.

If you find yourself in a course for which you lack the necessary background, immediately seek help.

II. Take Notes and Use Them

Take notes as you watch the lecture. Use them to answer the following questions.

1. Why is it important to understand how American government works?

    _____

2. What are the three branches of American government? _____

    _____

3. What do some sociologists call the "fourth branch"?_____

    _____

4. Similar to British Parliament, what structure does the Legislature have?

    _____

5   What are the two parts of the Legislature? _____

    _____

6. Where does the Legislature get its authority? _____

    _____

7. What two general kinds of powers does it have? _____

    _____

8. How long are the terms for Senators? _____

9. How long are the terms for Representatives? _____

10. What is the nickname for a legislator who is good at making deals and

    getting things done? _____

11. Where does the Executive Branch get its authority? _____

_____

12. What position does the President hold with the military? _____

_____

13. Who must the President consult? _____

14. What do we call this system? _____

_____

15. Which branch can take action most quickly? _____

16. What characteristics might describe four different kinds of Presidents?

_____

_____

17. Where does the judicial branch get its authority? _____

_____

18. What are the three types of courts? _____

_____

19. What is the function of the Supreme Court? _____

_____

20. What is the assignment for next time? _____

_____

III. Outline an Essay

Here are directions for a writing assignment based on Mr. Morales's lecture:

In a five-paragraph essay, explain the structure of American government.

Strategies for this assignment:

1) *Understand the question.* What are you being asked to do?

This question calls for you to repeat the ideas presented in Mr. Morales' lecture. You must write a well-organized summary in which you demonstrate that you have learned the material.

In contrast, other essay questions may not ask for a summary of what was presented. They may ask for your original opinions and ideas. Be sure you follow directions and answer the question asked.

If the professor asks for an apple and you give him an orange—even if it is a delicious one—it is still not the apple required, and you will be likely to get a low grade.

2) *Organize your decision-making process.*

Instead of trying to do everything at once, first make an outline in which you decide what to say and when to say it.

Since the essay needs three body paragraphs, and the government has three branches, let each branch be the focus of a body paragraph. As you create your outline, use your notes to fill in the information.

3) *Let your outline be your map.*

After you outline your ideas and you feel ready to compose your essay, write one paragraph at a time. Use your outline to help you stay organized and focused as you craft well-connected sentences.

Now, by yourself or working with a partner, create an outline for this essay assignment. You may refer to your notes.

IV. Things to Do and Discuss

1. The Bill of Rights is the nickname for the first ten amendments to the U.S. Constitution. The Constitution has been amended twenty-seven times. Have each student select an amendment, research its meaning, and report back to the class.

2. If you are familiar with the government of another country, prepare a brief presentation explaining how it is organized. In addition to speaking, try to include objects for your classmates to see and handle.

3. "It's a free country," Americans often say. What does "freedom" mean? Have each student write a definition on a slip of paper. Put all the slips in a basket, and then pull out someone else's. Read the definition, and then provide an example that you could use if you were planning an essay explaining that meaning of "freedom."

4. Select a current news event, and ask each student to bring to class stories about it from various sources, such as news magazines, national and city newspapers, web sites, and TV and radio networks. Include stories from international media. Compare the descriptions of the same event.

5. Witnesses in court must swear to "tell the whole truth, the full truth, and nothing but the truth." Consider what this promise means.

    Have you ever observed an accident, an unusual natural occurrence such as an earthquake or hurricane, or an athletic event, and discovered that you described it very differently than did other observers? In small groups, provide examples, and try to arrive at a definition of the "truth."

6. Select one or more controversial issues and organize a debate. State each issue as an affirmative opinion. One team will argue "pro" (yes) and the other "con" (no). Teams can consist of two to four members.

    If time permits, after the teams have argued their original viewpoints, have the debaters switch sides and argue the issue again, favoring the opposite point of view.

In secret ballot, the class members may vote to determine which team has argued their viewpoint(s) best.

7. Explain and discuss these sayings as they relate to government.

- A stitch in time saves nine.

- The squeaky wheel gets the grease.

- Live and let live.

- I scratch your back, and you scratch mine.

- "The buck stops here." (President Harry S Truman)

V. Write

1. Write the essay you planned in "III. Outline an Essay."

2. Write a letter explaining your opinion on a current political issue. Address it to a U.S. Senator or Representative, or to the editor of a newspaper or magazine.

3. The topics in "IV. Things to Do and Discuss" can be adapted and developed as compositions.

14

Henry the Fifth
Introduction to Literature

Javier Chapa

I. Read the Assignment

Professor Chapa's students are reading William Shakespeare's play **The Life of King Henry the Fifth**. The play contains five acts, each consisting of several scenes. The assignment for today's class is to study Henry's speech in Act Four, Scene Three.

Shakespeare lived and wrote four hundred years ago, so his English may seem quite different from what we use today. To make this scene easier to understand, in addition to reading it yourself, borrow an audio and/or video recording of the play from the library. Also, try role playing part of the scene and reading the speeches aloud.

As with all reading assignments, mark up the text. Read actively, responding to the play. Underline important phrases, put a question mark by words whose meanings you need to check, and write down your reactions to what the characters say.

In literature, the "setting" refers to the time and place in which the action occurs. In this play, King Henry is leading the English who are at war with the French in the early Fifteenth Century. The scene occurs in France just before a battle is about to take place.

Accompanying King Henry are Bedford, Exeter, Gloucester, Salisbury, Talbot, and Westmoreland, who are all British aristocrats.

The scene's line numbers do not begin with number one because only the part of the scene that Professor Chapa discusses is included here. The italicized names indicate the character giving each speech.

Westmoreland: O! that we now had here   20
But one ten thousand of those men in England
That do no work today.

King Henry: What's he that wishes so?

My cousin Westmoreland? No, my fair cousin: 24

If we are marked to die, we are enow

To do our country loss; and if to live,

The fewer men, the greater share of honor.

God's will! I pray thee, wish not one man more.   28

By Jove, I am not covetous for gold,

Nor care I who doth feed upon my cost;

It yearns me not if men my garments wear;

Such outward things dwell not in my desires: 32

But if it be a sin to covet honor,

I am the most offending soul alive.

No, faith, my coz, wish not a man from England:

God's peace! I would not lose so great an honor   36

As one man more, methinks, would share from me,

For the best hope I have. O! do not wish one more:

Rather proclaim it, Westmoreland, through my host,

That he which hath no stomach to this fight,   40

Let him depart; his passport shall be made,

And crowns for convoy put into his purse:

We would not die in that man's company

That fears his fellowship to die with us.   44

This day is called the feast of Crispian:

He that outlives this day, and comes safe home,

Will stand a tip-toe when this day is named,

And rouse him at the name of Crispian.   48

He that shall live this day, and see old age,

Will yearly on the vigil feast his neighbors,

And say, "Tomorrow is Saint Crispian:"

Then will he strip his sleeve and show his scars,   52

And say, "These wounds I had on Crispin's day."

Old men forget: yet all shall be forgot,

But he'll remember with advantages

What feats he did that day. Then shall our names,   56

Familiar in his mouth as household words,

Henry the king, Bedford and Exeter,

Warwick and Talbot, Salisbury and Gloucester,

Be in their flowing cups freshly remembered.   60

This story shall the good man teach his son;
And Crispin Crispian shall ne'er go by,
From this day to the ending of the world,
But we in it shall be remembered;   64
We few, we happy few, we band of brother;
For he today that sheds his blood with me
Shall be my brother; be he ne'er so vile
This day shall gentle his condition: 68
And gentlemen in England, now a-bed
Shall think themselves accursed they were not here,
And hold their manhoods cheap while any speaks
That fought with us upon Saint Crispin's day.

Enter Salisbury   72
Salisbury: My sovereign lord, bestow yourself with speed:
The French are bravely in their battles set,
And will with all expedience charge on us.   76

King Henry: All things are ready, if our minds be so.

Westmoreland: Perish the man whose mind is backward now!

King Henry: Thou does not wish more help from England, coz?

Westmoreland: God's will! my liege, would you and I alone,   80
Without more help, could fight this royal battle!

King Henry: Why, now thou hast unwished five thousand men;
Which likes me better than to wish us one.
You know your places: God be with you all!   84

II. Take Notes and Use Them

Take notes as you watch the lecture. Then, use them to answer the following questions.

1. What is the first theme in Henry's speech? _____

2. What is the second theme in the speech? _____

3. What is the third and most important one? _____

4. According to Mr. Chapa, what is one reason why people have children?

_____

5. What three examples does he give of people whose names have lived

on? _____

_____

6. What months were added because of two of those people? _____

_____

7. What are the odds for the upcoming battle? _____

8. Who does Henry say should go back to England? _____

_____

9. What does the good man do? _____

_____

10. When will the men's fame end? _____

III. Take a Stand

Professor Chapa's assignment is to write an essay explaining why you would or would not fight with Henry in order to attain immortality.

Notice that the assignment does not ask for a summary of the lecture. He wants you to write your own ideas.

Independently or with a partner, clarify your thinking by making two lists: one with reasons to fight with Henry, and one with reasons not to do so. Even if you already have an opinion on this topic, you can benefit from considering the opposite viewpoint. Creating two lists will help you define the important issues. A strong essay explains not only why you think what you do, but also why you reject an alternative.

IV. Things to Do and Discuss

1. For the essay assignment about being willing to fight with Henry, do you think Mr. Chapa will grade papers higher if the writers say they would fight for immortality? Why or why not?

2. When Mr. Chapa asks his students if any of them have brothers who are kings, several raise their hands. They are joking. In some schools, their behavior might be considered disrespectful. List at least three ways that Mr. Chapa sets the tone for his class, showing his students that informal interactions are OK.

3. Why should a math or science major have to take General Education courses in literature, and vice versa? Set up a debate with one side arguing to keep General Education requirements, and the other side arguing that courses in a student's major should be all that are required for a degree.

4. Many of Shakespeare's words have become so familiar that speakers are not even aware of the source. Explain and discuss the meaning of these famous quotes from Shakespeare's plays:

- "To be, or not to be—that is the question."
    Hamlet (Act Three, Scene One)

- "To thine own self be true."
    Hamlet (Act One, Scene Three)

- "The course of true love never did run smooth."
    Midsummer Night's Dream (Act One, Scene One)

- "O Romeo, Romeo! wherefore art thou Romeo?"
    Romeo and Juliet (Act Two, Scene Two)

- "All the world's a stage, and all the men and women merely players."
  As You Like It (Act Two, Scene Seven)

- "Friends, Romans, countrymen, lend me your ears!"
  Julius Caesar (Act Three, Scene Two)

- All that glitters is not gold."
  The Merchant of Venice (Act Two, Scene Seven)

V. Write

1. Compose an essay explaining why you would or would not fight with King Henry in order to attain immortality.

2. Any of the topics in "IV. Things to Do and Discuss" can be developed into essays.

15

Selecting Sources
Research

Heidi Holbrook

I. Get Ready to Research

Most college courses require that students write papers. Their length may range from a short personal reaction essay to an extensive research paper.

To write a research paper, you must gather information, organize it, and then present it in the appropriate format. Ms. Holbrook's lecture focuses on the first step: gathering information. She refers to the M.L.A., which stands for the Modern Language Association. **The M.L.A. Handbook** provides guidelines for standard research paper format.

As you do your research, note information not only about the topic, but also about your sources. M.L.A. guidelines specify the exact information needed and how to present it.

Ms. Holbrook assumes her students know how to use the internet. If you are at an American college but you are not familiar with the internet, visit your school's counseling center and ask where you can get basic instruction in how to work online. You may want to take an introductory course or learn independently at a computer lab on campus or at a public library.

II. Take Notes and Use Them

Take notes as you watch the lecture. Use them to answer the following questions.

1. What was assigned last week? _____

2. What is the topic? _____

3. List eight questions that should be answered. _____

_____

_____

_____

4. What are four examples of print sources? _____

_____

5. Which print sources are best? _____

_____

6. Which are not so good? _____

_____

7. If you can't check a source out from the library, how can you easily get

the information home? _____

8. What are three examples of information about magazines that will be

needed for M.L.A. format? _____

_____

9. What two criteria are important for books when you're researching a

career? _____

_____

10. Where in the book is a good place to check to see if there is information about a career? _____

11. What are some of the pieces of information needed for books listed in the bibliography? _____

_____

12. What else is an excellent research source? _____

13. Where can you get the most current information? _____

14. What are some good web sites to start with? _____

_____

15. When you find a good source online, what is the first thing you should do? _____

16. List at least three things that might reveal that a site is not very reliable. _____

_____

_____

17. Which addresses tend to be most reliable? _____

_____

18. What is the homework? _____

_____

III. Summarize

Write a summary that includes the main ideas covered in Ms. Holbrook's class. Identify the key points made, put them in your own words, and then write them in about ten to twelve well-connected sentences.

IV. Plagiarism

"Plagiarism" means presenting someone else's words or ideas as if they are your own. In a research paper, you are gathering ideas from many sources. It is dishonest and even illegal to copy others' work without giving credit for it. At most colleges, a student who submits a plagiarized paper receives a failing grade. M.L.A. guidelines provide the academic conventions for giving credit and thereby avoiding plagiarism.

Most college-level composition courses cover how to write research papers. If you are assigned a research paper before you have taken a class that explains standard formats, you may—

- Ask the instructor who assigned the paper to provide guidelines.

- Study the **M.L.A. Handbook**. It is available in libraries and bookstores.

- Search the internet for research paper guidelines based on M.L.A. format.

- Ask for help at your school's Writing Center or Lab.

- Ask for help from a tutor.

V. Things to Do and Discuss

1. A bibliography is a list of sources of information on a particular topic (*biblio* refers to "book," and *graphy* refers to "writing"). Many research papers conclude with a bibliography or a list of sources that are cited in

the paper.

For researching a career, list as many types of information sources you can think of such as books, magazines, journals, etc. Ask each student to choose one of those types and find out the bibliographic information needed for each of those kinds of sources. Report back to the class. Many sites on the internet explain M.L.A. guidelines, or you can refer to the **M.L.A. Handbook**.

2. Find the following information about a career of your choice:

   • What major prepares someone for that career?
   • What college degree is needed?
   • What is the outlook for jobs?
   • What is the starting salary?
   • What are the opportunities for advancement?

Now, choose a partner. You will interview each other. Ask the questions below and note the answers in the blanks provided. Summarize the information given by your partner. Then, in your own words, present it to the class.

a. What career interests you? _____

b. What major prepares someone for that career? _____

c. What college degree is needed? _____

d. What is the outlook for jobs? _____

e. What is the starting salary? _____

f. What are the opportunities for advancement? _____

_____

3. Have you written a research paper? Explain in small groups or to your class what the topic was, and how you conducted your research. What advice would you give to someone writing a research paper for the first

time? If you have not written a research paper, describe the longest paper you have ever written. What did you learn from the experience?

4. Just as knowledge and information change, so do jobs and professions. With a partner, list at least five jobs of the past that no longer exist, and five jobs that have only recently been created.

5. Explain and discuss the following sayings that relate to the acquisition of knowledge.

- Curiosity killed the cat.
- A little knowledge is a dangerous thing.
- The more you know, the more you know you don't know
- Question authority.

VI. Write

1. Write a paper about a career that interests you. Answer the questions listed in topic one in "V. Things to Do and Discuss."

2. "To paraphrase" means to put something into your own words. Select a short article about a career that interests you. Summarize it in your own words. At the end, write the information about the source using the M.L.A. guidelines for an item in a bibliography.

3. If you won a scholarship that would support you for a year while you researched any subject, in a paper explain what you would study and why.

4. Although "research" suggests serious work by mature students and scholars, even young children conduct investigations in their own ways. Write a paper explaining something you researched as a child: what you wanted to find out, what you did, and what you learned.

16

A Student Project
Service Learning

Justin Imamura

I. Service Learning

Service Learning gives students the opportunity to move beyond the classroom and put into practice some of the theories they have been studying. Students learn from the hands-on experience, and the community benefits from their work.

In Justin Imamura's class, students were given a list of community agencies that wanted student volunteers. The projects required a minimum of twenty hours' worth of work outside the class. Students gave the instructor brief written reports about their experiences, and they presented oral reports to the class.

Instead of a lecture by a professor, this unit shows one student's description of his project.

II. Evaluate the Presentation

Service learning helps students link their academic courses with real world experiences. This exercise will help you do the same.

Evaluating people's performance helps you to improve your own, for you become more familiar with the criteria for evaluation. College graduates often do not begin on the bottom rung of the ladder in the work world. Like other employees, they are evaluated by their supervisors, but they may be responsible for evaluating other workers as well.

Completing the following form will give you practice in making an evaluation; in this case, you will evaluate an oral presentation.

To be an effective evaluator, remember to —

• note both strengths and weaknesses. People who hear only criticism are likely to suffer hurt feelings, and they may become defensive. Make your criticism as supportive as possible. Think of yourself as a coach who is trying to improve a team member's performance.

• be honest but kind. Use "I" statements rather than "you" statements, such as "I was confused by...." rather than "You were confusing...."

Watch Justin Imamura's presentation once, and then rewind the tape. The second time you see it, apply the following criteria for evaluation. Underline "yes" or "no" to indicate your judgment regarding each statement. Then, write as many specifics as you can to explain the basis for your answers. In the professional world, employees usually have a right to see their evaluations, to ask for clarification where needed, and to challenge any criticisms they do not think are fair.

Compare your comments with those made by your classmates.

The first one is filled in to serve as an example.

1. The speaker said where he did the project.

   <u>yes</u>   no

comment: *He said he did it at the Youth Commission, a nonprofit organization for young people. I like the way he further explained the organization by comparing it to city government.*

2. The speaker explained what his overall task was.

   yes   no

comment: _____

_____

_____

3. The speaker listed some of the specific activities he did to complete the task.

yes   no

comment: _____

_____

_____

4. The speaker explained research he needed to do.

yes   no

comment: _____

_____

_____

5. The speaker explained written materials he prepared.

yes   no

comment: _____

_____

_____

6. The speaker explained who he contacted in order to complete his task.

yes   no

comment: _____

_____

_____

7. The speaker explained how long it took him to do the work.

    yes   no

    comment: _____

    _____

    _____

8. The speaker explained how the project ended.

    yes   no

    comment: _____

    _____

    _____

9. The speaker responded well to any questions from his classmates.

    yes   no

    comment: _____

    _____

    _____

10. The speaker used effective speaking skills such as making eye contact, handing out supplementary materials, showing enthusiasm for his work, etc.

    yes   no

    comment: _____

    _____

    _____

• Justin has been invited to give his presentation to another class. Please give him general advice about what he should do the same next time, and what he might want to do differently:

_____

_____

_____

III. Things to Do and Discuss

1. Students are expected to learn from each other as well as from the professor. With a partner, based on Justin's example, create a list of ideas you gained about things to do and not to do when giving a presentation. Compare your list with those of your classmates.

2. Have each student prepare a brief explanation about something s/he learned while working either as a paid employee or as a volunteer. Before anyone presents, create an evaluation plan:

(a) Develop criteria for evaluating the presentations. You may get ideas from the lists created in discussing topic one, as well as from section "II. Evaluating a Presentation." Creating your own evaluation criteria will give you the opportunity to consider what factors are important in giving a clear, thorough, and effective presentation on this topic which calls for students to explain something they learned when doing a job.

Also, decide whether you want the evaluators to remain anonymous.

(b) Based on your criteria, create an evaluation form to be used for all the presentations. You might model it on the form in "II. Evaluating a Presentation." Customize it to suit your needs.

(c) Create a self-evaluation form for each presenter to give to the instructor.

(d)   Have the students give their presentations. After each one, classmates and the instructor fill out the evaluation forms, and the presenter fills out the self-evaluation form.

(e)   Your instructor may want to look over all the forms, and then give them to the presenter.

3.   A common expression says that "Experience is the best teacher," but rarely can experience take the place of formal education. Working with a partner, list examples of things that can best be learned by doing and those that can best be learned by studying in school. In what instances do the two overlap?

IV. Write

1.   Imagine that a new student is nervous about giving a presentation in class. In an essay, explain how to give a good presentation. You may use any topic as your example.

2.   Write an essay describing something you learned while working either as a paid employee or as a volunteer.

3.   Write an essay explaining how to be an effective evaluator.

4.   In a paper, describe a Service Learning opportunity you would like to have and why.